Celebrate the Joy in Each Moment!

JOY BRINGERS

Vickie D. Torrey

Copyright © 2011 Vickie D. Torrey

All rights reserved. No part of this book may be used or reproduced by any means, graphic, electronic, or mechanical, including photocopying, recording, taping or by any information storage retrieval system without the written permission of the publisher except in the case of brief quotations embodied in critical articles and reviews.

Balboa Press books may be ordered through booksellers or by contacting:

Balboa Press
A Division of Hay House
1663 Liberty Drive
Bloomington, IN 47403
www.balboapress.com
1-(877) 407-4847

Because of the dynamic nature of the Internet, any web addresses or links contained in this book may have changed since publication and may no longer be valid. The views expressed in this work are solely those of the author and do not necessarily reflect the views of the publisher, and the publisher hereby disclaims any responsibility for them.

ISBN: 978-1-4525-3283-7 (sc)

Library of Congress Control Number: 2011902649

Any people depicted in stock imagery provided by Thinkstock are models, and such images are being used for illustrative purposes only. Certain stock imagery © Thinkstock.

Printed in the United States of America

Balboa Press rev. date: 4/19/2011

To my mother Eunice Steele Torrey who lives deep in my soul and makes each breathe I take life giving. You are still with us Mama.

To my father Thelbert Torrey who inspires me to live my Life magnificently. I love you both.

Contents

Illustrations v
Foreword vii
Acknowledgments ix
Part I: Celebrate the Joy in Each Moment 1
    Joy Bringers 1
    I Hear a Symphony 6
    Laugh with Me 10
    I See the Sea 14
    Wait a Minute… 18
    Bumper Stickers Rock! 23
    Forgiveness 26
    Saying Goodbye to the Body 29
    Manifest Your Great! 33
    Service 37
    Celebrate! 40
    Going South 43

Part II: Healing Affirmations 48
    Healing Is a Journey 48
    Healing with Colors 49
    Affirmations 50
    Healing Colors—7-Days 50

About the Author 67
Meet the Artists 68
Bibliography 71

Illustrations

Two Cats	Flavio Zabotto
Red Hibiscus	Flavio Zabotto
Fat Dog	Flavio Zabotto
Orange Fish	Flavio Zabotto
Blue Cat	Flavio Zabotto
Brown Turtle	Flavio Zabotto
Yellow Red Hibiscus	Flavio Zabotto
Peace Dove	Flavio Zabotto
Parrot	Flavio Zabotto
Bird of Paradise	Flavio Zabotto
Orange Cat	Flavio Zabotto
Brasilian Animals	Flavio Zabotto
Vase of Flowers	Flavio Zabotto
Healing Tree Meditation	Cynthia J. Allison

Foreword

It began with a warm sensation in my heart center that would not fade away. In fact, it grew. Then the question came, "How can I serve more?" It was persistent and very clear. The clarity and persistence of the question became a familiar friend. Sometimes it appeared when I opened my eyes at sunrise. It often showed up when I was walking in nature or enjoying the warmth of the sun.

And yet, I received no answers. I lived with this friendly visitor for almost two years. The strangest sensations accompanied the question. It brought with it feelings of anticipation, uncertainty, gratitude and reverence. It came with more puzzles than answers.

So, much to my surprise, in the midst of a walking meditation I heard the answers clearly. Write. Write and teach about your experiences. Write in Brazil! Who knew that when the answer finally came it would help me find the home of my heart—Brazil. And finding Brazil would lead to the most extraordinary adventures of my life! In the past few years I have opened my heart and arms wide to Life. I have not only embraced Life, but recognized that there really is no separation. I am Life and Life is me.

Since my move to Brazil, my writing has blossomed. On November 11, 2009 I launched my ebook entitled: *Live! Love! Heal! Abundant Life Affirmations*. Liveloveheal.org is an interactive site of healing spiritual affirmations accompanied by the breathtaking art of Brazilian artist Flavio Zabotto.

My beautiful daughter Serena read the affirmations called me and suggested that I add stories to the book. Others agreed. A few months later I was in retreat in the Warshauer family beach house in Wrightsville Beach, N.C. writing stories that inspired the affirmations. Waking up to the ocean facing my bedroom window, walking the beach every morning and hearing the sweet sounds of sea gulls inspired me deeply. It was a perfect fit because the other affirmations were written on the beaches of Costa Rica and Brazil. That's how *Joy Bringers* was born.

It is my wish that you see yourself in my stories because I am You and You are Me. There is no separation. These affirmations and stories spiritually expand and inspire beyond religious, socio-economic, cultural beliefs or even politics. We are from one Divine Creator, one Divine Source. This source of All-Life is known by many names by many people. What matters is that we recognize this union of spirits, this Oneness.

The last chapter contains fifty-six daily affirmations charged with the healing power of colors. We have all been uplifted, inspired, calmed or even healed by the marvelous colors that make up our universe. Just walk into a room filled with the sunny color of yellow and your emotions lighten and you feel happier. That is the magic of color. Use these simple affirmations for self-healing. There is amazing power in simplicity.

May you live peace, grace, abundance and Joy beyond your dreams. You are a Joy Bringer and it is time for you to reclaim your Joy!

Acknowledgments

I would like to first thank the Supreme Being, Divine Light, Unlimited Source, Fountain of Amazing Grace, which I call God for working through me to create this book.

I thank my mother, Eunice Steele Torrey, for encouraging me to write the books she saw in me and for being my first Spiritual Teacher. I send a heartfelt, warm, loving thank you to my other Spiritual Teacher, Linda Barnett.

Thank you to my father, Thelbert Torrey, Sr., for having such visionary ideas. To my brothers and their beautiful wives, Craig and Carla Torrey, Dennis-Salim and Asma Habeebullah, and Thelbert and Percillia Torrey, my sister Marilyn Torrey Rorie, and all my magnificent nieces and nephews, I love you on a grand scale.

Much love and eternal thanks to the Laura Alberta Steele Ballard, Vivian Steele Jones, Cora Steele, Sadie Steele Smith, and the Torrey women; Estelle Torrey McNeil, Luberta Torrey Campbell, Jetha Torrey Williams, Rosa Lee Torrey, Clara Bell Torrey, and Corine Torrey, whose loving attention and guidance inspired me to do my best at all times.

To my best friend, soul mate, spiritual sister of over 52 years, Barbara Armstrong White, I offer deep love and gratitude for you being a necessary part of my life.

My life is always exciting and astoundingly interesting with my posse of best friends, Annette Deltac, Reginald M. Edrington, Lorene Goins, Freddie Hubbard, Barbara Jefferson, Doris Johnson, James McNair, Kwame Motilewa, Phyllis Nadel, Michael A. Porter, Marnita Piersawl, Tammy H. Ratliff, Patricia Rogers, Steven K. Washington, and W. Troy Watson.

My Fayetteville posse Jesse White, Betty Malloy, Noreda Hess, Louise Roseborough, Dr. Patricia Robeson, Tisha Musser, Deborah Baker, Paula Williams, and Jo-Ann Borden. You Rock!

A warm and loving thank you to photographer, Noreda Hess for her amazing photos of me. You capture my energy perfectly Noreda!

There is tremendous power in spiritual sisterhood. You see my Light and I see yours. Thank you deeply Cynthia Calderwood, Tricia Richardson and Andrea Peinado.

My international friendships continue to flourish. I want to thank my Brazilian friends for all of your wonderful love and support. Paula and Al Alonso, Janete and Darryl Barringer, Sueli and Cristina Chibli, Alice and Charles Hixenbaugh, Lara Passos Kayanoki, Gicelia De Oliveira Marques, Edna Molinari, Diva Rodriques, Barbara Knocker and Ze Paulo de Paula e Silva, and Flavio Zabotto. Jill Berkana, Russell Bennett, Brenda Dragonne and all the students and staff of Costa Rica School of Massage Therapy, thank you for your enthusiastic support and loving energy!

To Qiana Martin, keep up your "Glamorous Soccer Life!" Live your dreams!

To Rossyln Crandell, I love hearing you say, "You Go Girl!" Thanks for believing in my writing.

My Carolinas Integrative Health Family of Charlotte, N.C. watched me grow, spread my wings and fly away… Thank God we are still loving each other. Thank you, Katie Lee, Cynthia Allison, Carol Strain, Wenhui Li, Phyllis Nadel, Anne Lee, Kim DeRhodes, Laurie Bremenour, Helga Armfield, Brooks Holland, Babak Makari, OD, Marcie DeMore, and Christy Johnson. To Dr. Russell Greenfield, MD., our Integrative Medicine pioneer, and Medical Director, thank you for being an inspiration and a true friend.

To my special friends from Carolinas Integrative Health, I offer my everlasting gratitude to you for encouraging me to write. Special thanks to Deb Smith, DeeDee Lisenby, Carol Lang, Barbara Pelham, and Nancy Fields.

My angels, Ingrid Haggerson, Susan Green, and Radhiah Jaaber: Thank you for watching over me and keeping me grounded in Divine Truth.

I send endless thanks out to Tom Warshauer and his wonderful family who opened up their hearts and beautiful home in Wrightsville Beach, N.C. The sounds and sights of the sea helped me write my stories.

Patrice Gaines, thank you for beautifully editing this book. I am so proud of your on-going and ever-growing accomplishments!

My heart beats with joy and gratitude for the beautiful art that vibrantly illustrates this book. Thank you, soul deep, Flavio Zabotto.

A special thank you to Brazilian photographer Ronald Kraag. Beautiful…

Cynthia J. Allison, my sister, daughter, teacher, friend…. Thank you for creating the Healing Tree for my healing color meditations. It was a delight working with you. You are a Joy Bringer!

To my beautiful daughters, Diarra Sabree Torrey Porter and Serena Joy Torrey Porter, my heart fills with such love and wonder that you should be in my life. You are my courage, my hope, my constant smile. I love you and thank you with all my heart. You are Joy!

My life is a melody of Abundant Joy!

In the quietness of my soul, I hear the pure sweet sounds of my inner Joy and I am healed.

Two Cats

Joy Bringers

OK, I am going to confess to you that I am a Joy Bringer. I have been in love with the state of Joy since I was a small child. Young children are born pure Joy Bringers and some are able to bring Joy for their entire lives. If I wasn't a Joy Bringer, then why would God have graced me with such a large smile and eyes that twinkle? I also came packaged with a giggle that is contagious and a heart that wants to love you up. That's just typical Joy Bringing.

I think that we can agree that babies are natural Joy Bringers. Babies can instantly recognize another Joy Bringer. Just lean over a new baby and smile. There is a connection that says, "Oh yeah, thank you for greeting me with your smile, you Joy Bringer you." And then the giggling begins.

It is easy to recognize the adult who is a Joy Bringer. We recognize each other instantly too. It starts with that smile. Then there comes the laughter. You just met, yet you are laughing together just from pure recognition. Delightful! You may also notice that we chuckle to ourselves a lot. Perhaps because life can be very funny at times.

Joy Bringers know how to laugh at themselves and move through the embarrassment of a wrong decision, poor timing, or whatever the world may throw at us. We believe that you have unlimited opportunities to change your day for the better. You can always start your day again with a positive perception.

We also think the very best about you. We are always looking for and finding the pure soul that you are. We can compassionately strip you of untruths about yourself and give you supportive and encouraging words to help you move through your healing times. Joy Bringers change family patterns and help create a future that is no longer mired and stuck in old family pains and stubborn mistruths.

I remember being about 9 or 10 years old, swirling and giggling in our front yard. I was finding Joy in the sensation of the wind against my skin and the warm sun bathing me in its radiance. My uncle, who was observing me, came up and gave me a life-changing message. He had spent time in Africa on a work assignment. This uncle had actually lived in a village and participated in the daily activities of the tribe.

"You have a lot of African in you!" he exclaimed. Well, I wasn't sure what he meant because our orientation to the Motherland consisted of re-runs of Tarzan and Jane movies. Oh, and maybe a few very natural pictures in the *National Geograhic*. I was not sure where he was going with that thought…

He continued to explain, "You are like the villagers who awaken in the morning with drumming to celebrate the day. They drum and dance when the men come back from a successful hunt or a bountiful harvest. They celebrate the birth of a child. And they even drum and dance to end the day."

"Wow!" I thought, "Take me to Africa! I am coming home!"

At that very moment I chose to be a Joy Bringer in my family. Every family needs at least one! Are you your family's Joy Bringer?

Imagine such a powerful connection to God's bounty. Imagine such gratitude and praise for being able to be alive another day. To know you are an important part of Divine Flow. To live with this deep sense of honor for life, embracing life fully in Joyful anticipation.

You probably are thinking that being a Joy Bringer is an easy job. Well, sometimes it is very easy. Feelings of love, Joy, bliss, optimism, compassion and excitement are all part of our spiritual package. These attributes exist in each and every one of us. Implied in being a Joy Bringer is the ability to consistently clear and cleanse your spiritual energy of old hurts, abuses, or injuries. It means living in the now with an awareness of the beauty that is right in front of your face.

What makes it not so easy is the unloving energy that other people sometimes direct toward you. Although Joy Bringers neutralize ugly, malicious actions with compassion and love, we are still experiencing human emotions. Why would a Joy Bringer be under attack? Perhaps the other person is suffering, in pain, feeling insecure, or possibly threatened by all this celebration.

You can only fake true celebration for a short period of time. The doubts, self-hate and insecurities begin to show themselves and the Joy Bringer may be the first to get the angry, sharp words or the devaluing of the celebration.

Never fear. Joy Bringers can find comfort in others just like them. The numbers are growing. More people are clearing and cleaning their spiritual energies and accepting Joy back into their lives. There are more wonderful groups and organizations now whose purpose is to help heal men, women, and children who have been neglected, abused, or wounded. There are many Circles of Love that openly profess and support the truth that healing our wounded is the only way we will save this world.

Maybe in reading these words you will recognize and honor the Joy Bringer inside of you. Begin your healing journey and open yourself up to God's Light and Love. Practice forgiveness for yourself and others in your life. Just be grateful that you are here now expressing God's love to all you meet.

I am happy to know that you can return to Joy. I trust that you will find peace in your soul and that you will appreciate all the good that is yours to claim. Remember, we are all born with love, Joy, bliss and excitement in our souls. I believe that you will reclaim those beautiful attributes for yourself. We Joy Bringers are holding you in Joy and Love. Hey that's what we do. We Bring the Joy!

Affirmations

I awaken each day to the wonder of Unlimited Possibilities!
It is a joy to know that each day holds more wonderful new experiences for me.

My life is a melody of Abundant Joy!
In the quietness of my soul, I hear the pure sweet sounds of my inner Joy and I am healed.

Here in this moment, I allow myself to experience Joy!
What state do I live in? The state of Spiritual Joy.

I am conscious of my oneness with creative life force energy and I manifest Joy in my life now!

I breathe in deeply to prepare myself to go within. Deep within me is a Divine Fountain of love, joy, peace, and beauty.

Red Hisbiscus

I Hear a Symphony

My friend Lara had invited me to stay with her family in Salvador, Bahia, Brazil for the fourth time and this time I was going! This year all the stars were aligned and I was actually going to Bahia! My excitement was barely containable. I have wanted to visit this place of cultural importance for Brazil for many years!

What I did not know was that we would be spending time in Chapada, Bahia, before I could settle in for my Salvador experience. I am open to the flow and I trusted that God would continue to guide me through this Brazilian adventure. And I love Lara, so I knew it would be fun. Seven of us headed for Chapada. Our party consisted of me and Lara's family members.

Chapada is a place of mystery and ancient secrets. I hiked and cooled my feet in water that was golden yellow. I was amazed and awed by all the natural wonders that this city has to offer. And then it happened….

On our second day, we went hiking into the caverns. Our guide carried an oil lantern and led us deeper and deeper under the earth. We were amazed by the beauty of the stalagmites and all the wonderful rock formations caused by thousands of years of water activity. Deeper we went with just the lantern to light our way. We trusted that our guide knew the way and would return us to the surface safely.

We rounded a corner and before us were perfect stone seats carved by nature. Our guide motioned for us to be quiet and take a seat. He then blew out his lantern and hurled us into total darkness. There was no light in sight. Just blackness.

I took a deep breath and grounded myself. I was not sure what was coming next. My spirit said, "Peace be still." That's my personal message that something profound is about to happen.

I allowed myself to connect with the emptiness and the blackness. Breathing in and out, I opened myself to receive. And then I heard it. Honestly, my first reaction was that some tour agency had piped flute music in for the tourist to have an extra treat during the exploration. I listened deeply and my soul recognized the truth. This was no man-made performance. This was a perfect symphony composed by wind, water and rock! It was God's Symphony. It sounded like beautiful flute music. The melody was timeless, eternal.

I felt tears of Joy flow down my face. My breathing deepened and I just listened. Here in this stillness… here in this darkness was pure Bliss. I felt honored to be listening to this Divine concert. My body was swaying to the rhythm. I was entranced by the sheer awesomeness of the moment. It was spiritually transforming and I accepted it.

Then our guide relit his lantern. Lara's sister and I were shocked to find that only the two of us heard the symphony. Some of our group was distracted by the absence of light. Others gave into normal distractions that occur when we try to sit still for a moment.

It takes a little practice to remove yourself from distractions, yet you owe it to yourself. We each have a symphony inside of us. Perhaps years of busyness have muffled your hearing. Or maybe you distract yourself because you are afraid of what you might hear in your stillness. It takes courage to open oneself up to the spiritual well within, to quiet the inner talk and the outer distractions. But it is worth the spiritual work.

God has a perfect symphony waiting for you.

Affirmations

I welcome this opportunity to clear my mind of distractions and inner talk. My Divine Symphony awaits me and I am grateful!

In the still, deep recess of my soul I find Bliss and Divine Love.

The Sea of my Soul is Calm.
I am blissfully afloat in a world of solitude, calmness, and perfect peace.

I celebrate each breath!
Counting each breath, I find supreme peace in my heart.

Laughing connects us soul to soul.

Come laugh with me. Breathe in the sweet air of Joy and know that our spirits have touched.

Fat Dog

Laugh with Me

Laughter is a powerful healing tool. Laughter has been documented to increase breathing, increase heart rate and encourage a deeper state of relaxation. Numerous studies have shown the benefits of laughing. They have supported the belief that laughing releases natural neurotransmitter substances in the brain (endorphins) that help override pain and just make us feel better. Laughing heals.

Most living things are attracted to laughter energy. Children, pets and even plants need happy energy for healthy growth. Organizations like The Wellness Community support the use of laughter and humor for both the cancer patients and the care providers who come in for health-related services.

Most patients who are experiencing chronic health conditions find themselves searching for that physician or health practitioner who is quick to smile and quick to laugh. It just feels good being around someone who has happy energy!

On an emotional level, laughing cleanses away feelings of sadness, despair and hopelessness. If you can see a small bit of humor in an otherwise serious situation, you open up to the possibilities of being non-judgmental and compassionate to yourself and others. When you can laugh, you can love!

Some people believe unconditional love takes a whole lot of laughter. Unconditional love happens when you are able to allow the other person or the situation to just be. It means that you are placing no conditions on them in order for love to be given. Unconditional love says that you get rid of your judgments and pre-existing perceptions. You are open to all quirks and eccentricities. Our quirky behavior is rich in opportunities to laugh at ourselves and laugh with others.

At the first opportunity, try laughing with someone. Just pick someone who *needs* to laugh or maybe a person who *loves* to laugh. For that moment make them your laughing buddy. Laugh deep from your belly. Watch as other people start to join in even though they don't know why you are laughing. We all need at least one person to be our laughing buddy!

When we laugh together we mingle our spiritual essences. The essence of Joy that is the purest form of our souls flows out to each other and we share Divine Life. Maybe this is why more and more religious organizations and churches are enjoying that special minister, rabbi, priest or imam who can inspire and teach with laughter. God is Joy.

So, breathe deeply and share a laugh. Be the first to smile. Pass the Joy forward.

Affirmations

Laughter is rebirth!
Laughter flows through my body, strengthening, rejuvenating and healing me.

Laughter renews the spirit, enlivens the soul and heals the heart!

Laughing is Joy turned inside out!

Laughter is like the wind of change within your soul. It shakes things up, moves things around and puts things in their proper places.

I see the sea and the sea in me is calm.

I see the star and the star in me is brilliant.

I see the moon and the moon in me is luminous.

Orange Fish

I See the Sea

I was strolling along Samara Beach and I just started chuckling to myself. I thought, "What a wonderful world we live in." Samara Beach is one of the most beautiful beaches in Costa Rica. The waves can be fierce and a little bit tricky for surfers or calm and peaceful, which is perfect for swimmers. It just depends on the tides, the ebb and flow….

I had just finished teaching class for today. It was an absolute dream to be in Costa Rica and to teach at Costa Rica School of Massage Therapy. The students were open, enthusiastic and grateful for the opportunity to learn about therapeutic touch and to just as importantly, learn about themselves.

On this day, the tides were very strong and powerful. I laughed because I am reminded that there is no separation between me and the sea. God has made both of us as changeable and predictable as we can imagine. In fact, it is our imagination that helps us grow spiritually. We as human beings could not grow and expand without our ability to imagine and to be creative.

Walking along the beach triggered a very special life-changing memory. My mother was extremely frightened of the thunder and lightening. So, whenever we experienced a severe thunderstorm, my mother hid all five of us in the closet and under the beds. I never questioned why she did this, it was just expected of us to obey her when she said hide.

For many years I carried around this fear of storms and although I did not run for cover, I was clearly full of fear. I was in my senior year in college and was spending time with a soul mate. Suddenly that day we began to experience one of the most ferocious storms imaginable. I shook and cringed. I was clearly terrified.

Then my friend did the most compassionate thing for me. He held my face in both of his hands and made me look into his eyes. Next he asked me a question: "Are you afraid of me?"

"Of course not!" I exclaimed.

He continued, his eyes staring into mine. "Well," he said, "I Am the Thunder and the Lightening. Have no fear."

It was a spiritual message that touched my soul deeply. From that pivotal moment, I have seen myself completely connected to all that is nature. If he is thunder and lightning, then so am I. We are all expressions of the Creator. The sea, the sun, the wind, the stars, and the trees all express the beauty that is Divine Light.

All of the creatures, both big and small, are part of this Divine expression too. We, as human beings, are beautiful expressions of God's creative light. We truly are all One.

So when I see the sea, I see me. When I see the stars twinkling in the sky, I see me. And guess what? I see you as the sea too!

With this new knowledge, I sat down on the beach one day and watched the sea and these affirmations emerged from my heart. Use them to help you appreciate how beautiful and powerful you are. Let them flow into your cells and renew your spirit. When you see that beautiful tree, know that you mirror its gracefulness and timelessness. Say to yourself, "I am that beautiful tree with the bright red flowers. Look at how Divine Beauty is expressing through me!"

You are the tree, the sea, the wind, the sun, and even all of the animals. You are beautifully and purposefully made.

Affirmations

I see the sun and the sun in me is passion.
I see the sun and sun in me is unlimited consciousness.

I see the star and the star in me is radiant.
I see the star and the star in me is visionary.

I see the tree and the tree in me is life-sustaining.
I see the tree and the tree in me is solace.

I see the moon and the moon in me is watchful.
I see the moon and the moon in me is acceptance.

Touch your children with care, nurture their young spirits, listen with compassionate hearts, and let them know that you cherish them.

Blue Cat

Wait a Minute...

Wait a minute.... Who is that fine man walking up the street? Tall, lean and handsome. And then I hear my name coming out of his beautiful mouth. "Is that Joseph?" I think.

Sure enough, it was my very first official boyfriend. We had not seen each other for over 40 years and the brother looked fantastic! Wow! Talking about maturing beautifully, this man still had the ability to make me grin just like a little girl.

Joseph started that kind of catch-up conversation that people have when they haven't seen someone for years. I am sure that there were gaps in the storytelling and I am certain that the gaps were intentional.

I listened with full attention because I really did want to know how his life had been. You see, Joseph was 13 years old and I was 11 when he asked me to be his girlfriend. I was very shocked and secretly thrilled that such an attractive guy wanted to spend time with me. Joseph actually thought I was cute.

Joseph was extremely affectionate. He loved to hold my hand, hug me, and just sit on the porch and talk to me about what was going on in his life. My emotions were in turmoil. You see, Joseph was offering me something that was very unfamiliar to me: positive male attention, affectionate touch and a deep appreciation for me as a lovely young lady.

My father was a very good provider. During my childhood there was not much time for the *"Father Knows Best"*, pseudo-home life in our family. Often my father and mother had to work in separate cities in order to provide for me and my four siblings.

In retrospect, I know my father did the best that he could, but there were no father-daughter kisses on the cheek, cuddles, or talks about life and boys. This left me totally unprepared for any type of male attention or affection. I was adrift in a sea of pre-teen anxiety, excitement and just plain fear. So, I did what any self-respecting, frightened out of her mind adolescent girl would do. I sabotaged the relationship.

To say that Joseph was not happy is an understatement. In fact, when he saw that he could not change my mind and get me to continue with our growing romance, he refused to speak to me for years. That is a pretty neat trick considering that we lived on the same street! What Joseph did not know was that in my mind he represented my father who I missed dearly.

Our minds do an unusual little thing which the world of psychotherapy calls transference. We unknowingly transfer our unresolved and unsettled emotions about our parents and other important people in our childhood onto someone else. I placed on Joseph's adolescent shoulders the responsibility of providing for me the perfect male relationship that I actually wanted from my father. Joseph was being held hostage to unattainable and certainly unrealistic expectations.

On the day that I ran into Joseph, as I listened to him talk, I slowly realized that this interrupted relationship had set the stage for many more moments of self-sabotaging. I also realized that I was not alone, that millions of women and men have turned away the possibilities of healthy nurturing relationships because of self-doubt and insecurities.

My soul smiled deeply as I realized that Joseph and I were back under the same tree in my front yard that sheltered our adolescent romance. I felt our circle of friendship was complete. Life had brought us back to ourselves a little older and hopefully wiser. I felt the same warmth from his special attention I used to feel long ago. When he caught my hand in his to bring me closer for a hug, my soul felt cherished.

I knew that I had forgiven myself for thinking that I was unlovable. I had forgiven the past hurts and untruths. I could live in this moment and know that I am an embraceable, lovable, spirit. As I forgave myself I freed my father, Joseph and all the other special men who came into my life. They were no longer being held hostage to my thoughts of shame, guilt and blame. I accepted the responsibility to love myself first.

Sometimes Life sends us a gift in the form of an old friend. The spiritual messages are powerful and clear. It helps us to understand that power of forgiveness. Perhaps life is also about being the love you want to receive and accepting the spiritual treasures of wisdom often gift-wrapped in pain.

We have to learn to love ourselves first before we offer our love to someone else. It is a beautiful charge to teach our children how to express love and how to accept healthy, loving attention. Honor the amazing spiritual lessons that our families gift us. Touch your children with care, nurture their young spirits, listen with compassionate hearts and let them know that you cherish them.

My story has a happy ending because of the power of spiritual counseling, somatic bodywork, self-forgiveness and good old fashioned girlfriend sessions. My willingness to begin my healing journey opened me to healthy experiences with men. I am grateful for the wonderful men who came into my life, who took the time and energy to help me understand and appreciate the beauty of my spirit. Joseph had traveled the world and loved many women and I could tell that he still thought I was cute. Oh yeah….

We parted that day each knowing that all was forgiven. Sometimes there is no need to extend the experience. It is enough to be in each other's energy for those moments to affirm that you have grown spiritually. That you hold no judgments, grudges or negative thoughts about the other.

Hopefully you also learned that by allowing yourself to love unconditionally you are able to change the ending of the story.

You have the power to change the story at any time you choose.

Affirmations

This experience is absolutely perfect for me!
There is only perfection in God. The Highest of High provides me with this perfect life experience in order to enlighten my spiritual path.

Don't be Afraid of the Dark!
My shadow places are wonderful places of loving insight to what needs to be healed in my life.

MOVE!
I shake myself from old habits, beliefs and thoughts. I move to a new vibration that is freer, livelier and richer.

This experience is about expansion.
My personal trials, tests and lessons are designed uniquely for my perfect spiritual growth. I open myself up to the wonderful possibility of spiritual expansion.

Lighten Up!

Your unique light is here to inspire, empower, awaken, and illuminate. Let your light shine on the path of others.

Brown Turtle

Bumper Stickers Rock!

My marriage was falling apart and there was nothing I could do. I had suggested counseling, struggled to be all he said he wanted, and still, my marriage was deteriorating.

After much soul-searching, I realized that I had to move out of my home. I needed to move to a protected space for my six-year old daughter Diarra and my unborn child. I wanted my new baby to grow in a happy and peaceful environment.

So, I moved. I was nine months pregnant. On moving day, my family and friends came to help me. I sat on an upside down bucket in the middle of all the moving activities and cried my heart out. In fact, we were all crying. The house was full of mixed emotions. Later that same night, Serena was born and I brought her home to apartment that was full of love and excitement.

Single parenthood was not something that I would have chosen for myself. I worked with single moms everyday and knew that it was not an easy job. My heart yearned for my husband to be there with us. Life had other plans for him.

As I struggled with my emotions, I began to feel increasingly sad, disappointed and just plain miserable. I was grieving deeper than I could have imagined. This nearly depressed state was so anti-me. I am usually the upbeat happy one. I am optimistic. I love to express Joy. Yet, here I was bordering on depression.

One day as I was driving through town, I noticed that the car ahead of me was going a little too slow for what I needed to do that day. I was driving and at the same time I was replaying over and over again how I could have kept my marriage alive. The more I hit the replay button in my mind, the sadder I became.

I finally looked up to see why the car in front of me was travelling at such a snail's pace. There, right in front of my eyes, was a bumper sticker. It said, "Misery Is Optional." Something clicked inside my spirit. Yes, it is so true that misery, depression, sadness, hurt feelings, are all options. They are all choices.

On that day, I chose to be happy. I chose to live a Joy-filled, spiritually enthusiastic life! I also chose to attract to me beautiful, prosperous, spirit enriching experiences and people. I thank the Divine for that bumper sticker!

Affirmations

I gratefully submit to God's Higher Intelligence!

All events flow from God!
Events happen in our lives to help us learn the Faith principle.

I grow under God's Loving Care!
I know that the Highest of High is at the Center of my Growth.

I don't have to do it alone!
Extraordinary events are in place now to connect me with the perfect people, things, and experiences to help me live my best life.

I forgive myself.

As I forgive myself, I experience clarity in my life. My spirit is filled with Divine Light that centers, guides and directs me. It clears my path.

Yellow Red Hibiscus

Forgiveness

Most of us think that forgiveness involves a one-on-one dialogue with the person who we want to forgive or who we feel needs to forgive us. There can occur at any point of our lives incidents that require forgiveness and healing. Forgiveness is a powerful healing channel.

Marianne Williamson in her popular book, *A Return to Love*, speaks of forgiveness as a change in our perception. She explains that when we forgive a person or a situation, a healing shift takes place. This shift is an alteration of perception or "how we hold that experience in our minds---how we experience the experience." As we change the way we think about the experience, we open the door for forgiveness.

If we can look at that person or incident with love and compassion, we can begin to change our perception and thus begin the process of healing through forgiveness. Most often when we feel slighted, abused, insulted, or wounded in any way, we focus on how we feel about the person or occurrence. We place our own beliefs and emotional attitudes on that person. This is called projection in the world of psychotherapy.

Sometimes open dialogue with the other person will reveal that they had no intention of hurting you! Maybe their biggest offense was not being considerate of how you would feel. Many times they were not being malicious but were just thinking of how it would affect or benefit them!

It is also important to remember to be in the present with our daily living. It is unhealthy and unproductive to drag around pass hurts and personal slights. Living in your now strongly implies that you rid yourself of those thoughts, behaviors, or attitudes that are not supporting the truth about your spirit. Divine Spirit is pure love and radiant light.

Forgiveness begins with changing our perception of how we move through life. Self-compassion and self-love are the first antidotes to a spirit that needs the healing touch of forgiveness. We have to perceive and think of ourselves as worthy of God's unconditional love. Reminding ourselves that we are The Beloved helps us to generate more love for ourselves and others.

Affirmations

I forgive myself!
I forgive myself for any past mistreatment of my body. I can now move forward with a loving heart knowing that I will treat myself well.

I no longer give guilt power in my life!
I replace guilty thoughts with thoughts of forgiveness, self-love and peace.

I wish the best for you!
Spiritual thoughts of love, peace, kindness and abundance that you send to others flow back to you strengthened and multiplied.

Soul Under Construction!
Watch out! Miracles are happening in my life. My soul is under construction and I am spiritually changing and growing every day.

*What Joy, what Light, what Perfect Peace!
I accept God´s Magnificent Love now!*

Peace Dove

Saying Goodbye to the Body

There comes a time when we must all transition from our bodies. In our human experience, death is inevitable. How we say goodbye to our bodies and how we feel about what happens next is probably one of our scariest challenges.

People perceive and believe many things about death and dying. Some people believe that once the body dies there is nothing else. They feel that you should live your best life everyday because nothing is promised after you die. Others believe that life is eternal and that our spirits leave the body and continue to do spiritual work into eternity. This ideology teaches that our spirits are constantly evolving.

The important thing is that you have a belief about death and dying that brings you some sense of peace and Joy. Being in a state of peace about death and dying simply means that you know that it will happen one day and that when you do die you can rest in the assurance that all is well. Feeling a sense of Joy about death and dying means you can now celebrate your life's passage in whichever form you choose to believe.

I was in Minas Gerais, Brazil recently visiting with close friends Sueli and Cristina. I really did think that I was on vacation, but somehow I ended up in a hospital room providing compassionate touch to a friend's father who was at the end-stage-of-life due to cancer. This man was a man of the earth. His whole life had been about growing and sustaining plants, trees or anything of the earth. He was into ecology and saving the planet.

On this day, he was struggling and fighting, trying to stay on the earth that he loved so passionately. I felt his energy and sensed that he would leave soon. I just wanted to help him shift his focus from struggling to acceptance. I also provided healing touch to the family members that were present in his room.

Early the next morning we received the news that he had died. Yet, something wonderful had happened for him before he slipped away. He and his grandmother had not spoken for nearly 20 years because of some personal slight or misunderstanding. When his grandmother came to visit him during his final moments, he grabbed her hand and held it. We were told that he died holding her hand. I would like to believe that he had finally felt his peace and Joy.

My mother had been experiencing a degenerative health condition for many years. She and I had spoken many times about death and dying. In the last conversation she and I had about dying, she admitted that she was afraid. We talked about the fear and it was one of our most beautiful moments. She asked me to read her favorite Bible verses and we sang some of her favorite hymns. I could see her reaching for her peace and accepting God's will.

A few months later, while I was in Brazil, I received the news that my mother had died. The story is that she woke up one morning and told my father that she was ready to go. The next day her heart stopped and her spirit was set free.

Often at end-stage-of-life people prioritize what is important in their lives. They may do their personal checklist to see if they have loved enough, given enough, or been enough of a blessing to their families, friends and to the world. Surprisingly when given a few days or weeks to live, your priorities take on a sense of purity. You strip away the unnecessary so that you can get to what is real and true in your life.

My uncle Edward was a man who saw life's complexities and was a genius at simplification. I called him the "wrap it up" man. He was that man who could listen to a two hour conversation and come in at the end to wrap up all the best points and leave you with one more thought to ponder. Uncle Edward had been experiencing a degenerative heart condition for several years. He finally had to live in a skilled nursing care facility with 24-hour medical attention. He was still alert and aware of everything that was happening in the world.

We went to visit him and discovered him literally surrounded by all of his favorites; Oreo cookies, Yahoo chocolate milk, Nehi Grape soda, and a bag of mixed candy bars. I teased him and asked how he was getting away with having all this contraband in his bedroom. He looked at me with a big smile and said, "Oh, it's going to be alright." Our eyes connected and I knew that he had been given permission to indulge himself. He had accepted his dying and he meant to go out satisfied with a sweet taste in his mouth.

I believe that the idea of leaving your body with a sweet taste in your mouth is the same as leaving in a state of grace. When you are at peace and have accepted the Joy of your passage, you grace yourself and your loved ones with a profound sense of serenity.

Affirmations

I release thoughts of grief, loss, sadness.
I fill my world with Radiant Joy and prepare my spirit for flight!

Counting each breath, I create a sea of peace and calmness within me now.
I breathe in this sense of one time; one space, and feel my spirit soar!

The separation between me and you is just an illusion.
We are together always.

Here in this sweet place of acceptance, I feel God's Loving Presence.

There is power in my imagination!

My thoughts are creative things that are always poised to bring about spiritual abundance, wisdom and joy in my life!

Parrot

Manifest Your Great!

As little girls, my best friend Barbara and I eagerly waited for the Sunday newspaper. We would take the Home and Garden section, find a quiet place, open the paper to the floor plans for the home of the week, and begin to re-create the home to our specifications. Sometimes we added another floor or made the living room a sunken space. We were always expanding the kitchen and adding bay windows and sun porches. We were spiritually manifesting our future homes.

Spiritual manifestation is one of our most talked about experiences. We are all manifesting our good at our personal comfort level. To manifest means to bring into your now what you think, desire, or live.

The experiences are wide open. If you are fearful and carry negativity around with you, eventually you will manifest negative and fearful experiences in your life. A spiritual teacher was once heard to say, "God says Yes to everything. There is not a *No* in God!" We, in our human experience, create the "No's" in our lives.

Just recently spiritual teachers from all walks of life went public on the power of The Law of Attraction. We were bombarded with information about how to attract your Good. The basic understanding is that we are manifesting every day of our life and that we attract to us what we think, feel and do.

What's important is to be spiritually grounded. This means that first you must understand that the Divine Creator is Unlimited. The Supreme Being is more than we can imagine. Yet, we have free will to imagine whatever we want! What works best for me is to imagine and leave a whole lot of room for the Creator in all his infinite wisdom to do all the upgrades. That's when the miracles are manifested!

Look around you and take an inventory of your manifestation skills. Are you experiencing a constant flow of good in your life? Are you depressed and feeling unloved? Do you see poverty all around you? Remember, the universe says Yes to everything, so if you are think poverty and lack, that's exactly what you get.

If you think that you are stuck in a job or relationship that you absolutely hate, you will continue to feel stuck until you change your mind and your perception about your situation. Here is an opportunity to drop a big load of Love on what you perceive to be a problem or issue. Love is the ultimate form of alchemy. Loving that situation or person makes you a spiritual alchemist.

Here's something else I have learned. You can only fake prosperity and abundance for a short time. Now hear me well. Sometimes you do have to fake it until you make it. What's important is that you really make it! Making it means that you have a spiritual understanding of how and why your manifestations are being birthed. It also means you have a deep sense of gratitude and Joy for the blessings that are flowing from the Divine Creator.

I have always loved visiting tropical islands. I have enjoyed crystal turquoise blue water and golden sunlit beaches for many years. The walls of my workspace were tastefully decorated with postcards and trinkets from my visits to the Caribbean. My friends and family told me they saw me living on a beautiful island.

I said, "No, not me!" But God said, "Yes!" And I submitted to His will. Now I live on a beautiful island named Ilhabela. It is located off the coast of São Paulo, Brazil. Ilhabela (which means beautiful island) is full of tropical foliage, waterfalls, beaches, natural trails, and importantly, my warm and wonder Brazilian friends who love and support me when I arrive ready to live, play and write.

More people are now rediscovering the power of imagery. Use your imagination and spiritually grounded best intentions to manifest your good. If you need visual energy to support your imagination, find colorful pictures for a visual representation of your desires. It speeds up the process of manifestation. Now, the most important part of this process is this: Surrender and Submit. The Divine Creator does not need you to micromanage.

Affirmations

With perfect awareness of my Divine Oneness with Source I manifest Joy, Peace, Love and Beauty in my life Now!

All things are manifested from one Perfect Divine Source. My awareness of my connection to Divine Source allows me to manifest all that I need perfectly in my life.

I deserve to live an abundant life!
Prosperity, wealth and abundance are my spiritual inheritance. I embrace abundant life now.

I open myself to unlimited Good!
I believe in infinite possibilities and abundant spiritual resources. God is constantly supplying all I need and more.

I am grounded in Spiritual Truth!

I know that I am one with Spiritual Truth and Divine Guidance. I am steady, calm, grounded and prepared to give the best service to others.

Bird of Paradise

Service

One of the most powerful purposes human beings can have is to be of service. To serve is to put someone else's needs at the forefront. It is to offer oneself as a light to guide another along their path. Service is about Light, whether your intention is to lighten a burden or to bring light (Divine Light) into unconsciousness.

To serve well is to be in a constant state of awareness and alertness in order to foresee the needs of others. Service is not only about Light, it is also about vision. To offer excellent service, you must first visualize an excellent result. Let's say you are serving a loved one who needs nurturing and caring attention.

When you are in an excellent state of service, you have already envisioned what they need and how you will lovingly supply it for them. You are alert to creative instruction. Your heart is open and through this beautiful center of love and compassion, you respond. "How can I serve?"

Something simple as cooking a meal for your aunt, who is now unable to cook for herself, becomes an act of reverence. Your inner vision sees her sitting and enjoying each delicious bite that you have lovingly prepared for her. Maybe you envision a beautiful tray setting with a small bud vase tucked full of her favorite flowers and special napkins.

Perhaps you plan to use her holiday china and silverware. You can envision her surprise. You hope to light up her day and when you place the tray down in front of her, you are rewarded by her eyes lighting up with Joy and gratitude.

Service that is heart-centered asks for nothing in return. The joy is in the giving. Each tiny step of preparation is filled with joy when it comes from the heart. Here is present moment in action. For each moment of preparation is filled with Divine Purpose.

Service and giving are sisters. Giving that is unconditional has unlimited spiritual returns. Unconditional giving also has no expectations. Giving is like the sea. The sea has no expectations for what it gives to us. It asks for nothing in return. The sea is a powerful force that excites, inspires, nourishes, calms, and enlightens us just by its existence. It gives beyond our imagination or comprehension. The sea is in an endless state of giving.

Our own acts of service and giving should be like the beautiful sea--, unexpected, constant, powerful, nurturing, abundant and unconditional. Be the sea.

Affirmations

I breathe in peace and tranquility.
I stop my work for a moment to breathe in and out. Each breath rejuvenates, re-charges and re-energizes me.

My co-workers enjoy working with me!
This Joy and enthusiasm that radiates from within me creates a wonderful working environment for me and my co-workers as we serve today.

My service is like the sea---constant, nurturing, loving and unconditional.

Each moment of service is filled with unlimited joy and Divine Purpose.

When we celebrate the moments in life, we create a higher vibration for ourselves and the world. Celebration opens the door to the deepest moments of self-love and self-awareness.

Orange Cat

Celebrate!

Suppose when you asked the universe, your spiritual teacher, the Divine Creator, what your purpose was, the reply came back, "Your purpose is to celebrate!" What emotions would you immediately experience? Sit quietly for a second and be in that moment.

Would your heart begin to thump with joyful excitement? Would you break out in a huge smile? Did your inner light feel like it had been switched on to mega watt?

Or would that simple sentence, inviting you to purposeful celebration cast you in a sea of confusion and uncertainty? Take this question into the center of your heart and allow yourself to hear the truth. To recognize all that life is-- peace, Joy, abundance and love-- is to be open to celebration. Don't you want that? It is your Divine Inheritance, so celebrate!

When we celebrate the moments in life, we create a higher vibration for ourselves and the world. Our celebration inspires others to do the same. It opens the door to the deepest moments of self-love and self-awareness. We become aware that we are all designed to express Joy. Being in a state of Joy leads us into celebration.

How can you bring more celebration into your life? Celebrate where you are right now. When you wake up in each morning celebrate that you woke up. Then give thanks by saying, "Thank you God for another beautiful day in Paradise." No matter where you might be at the moment, your celebration makes that present moment Paradise.

Give Joyful thanks to the abundance that surrounds you. It is always right there in front of you. The endless grains of sand beneath your feet express abundance. The flowers in all their colorful glory shout abundance. The wind whispers abundance in your ear. Even when hidden behind the clouds the sun is in a constant state of giving. It is there for us--warming, enlightening and encouraging us to express our Divine Light.

Celebrate that you can change your thoughts, actions or your habits at any time you desire. You don't have to stay stuck in unawareness or unhappiness. When you ground yourself emotionally you can create and re-create your good at any moment. Open yourself up to Life's possibilities.

Celebrate that you are success, abundance, prosperity, perfect health and love in action. You have all that you need and desire and much more. It is all part of your Divine Inheritance. Celebrate!

Affirmations

Life is celebration!
I am aware that life calls me to celebrate now.

Each moment is a special opportunity for me to celebrate Life!
I choose to live my life to the fullest, expressing Life in all its glory.

I celebrate each breath!
Counting each breath, I find supreme peace in my heart.

Celebrate the Zen moments!
I listen, breathe in, and absorb the beauty in my surroundings.

Thank you Divine Creator for another beautiful day in paradise....

Brasilian Animals

Going South

"Moving south!" my family and friends exclaimed. "Where? Atlanta, Georgia? Miami, Florida? Oh, I know, Arizona," they guessed, loudly. Cheers and other sounds of celebration filled the sunny kitchen.

I laughed at their hopeful expressions. Their responses were clear indications of places they really wanted to visit. I've traveled to countries in Europe and the Caribbean, but this was my first announcement of a move after 30 years of living and raising my daughters Diarra and Serena in Charlotte, North Carolina.

"No," I said with a wide smile. "Farther south—Brazil!" Both my daughters grew even more excited after hearing my destination. My sister, Mikki, who had lived in Europe for more than six years, cheered. Barbara, my best friend of 50 years, began an impromptu Carnival dance. Some of my other friends struggled with dismay, sadness, and anger. It is difficult to leave friendships that you nurture every day.

My decision to move began with two questions I asked in meditation and prayer: "How can I serve more? And: "How can I help more people?" The questions grew into a warm sensation around my heart, but for two years there was no answer.

So I continued to enjoy being one of the first two licensed massage therapists at Carolinas Integrative Health (CIH), a complementary health department at one of the largest regional hospitals in North Carolina and South Carolina. For CIH, I had left my position of 27 years as a social worker. Massage and healing touch called me, and leaving my social-work job was one of my best decisions. That first leap of faith took me out of a false sense of security into full-purpose living.

For the next four years my beloved family at CIH and I educated, inspired and facilitated healing of anyone who entered our doors. Thousands of medical professionals' and patients' lives were changed through the grace of compassionate touch and nurturing words. We celebrated and encouraged the unification of spirit, mind and body. I loved my work, family of co-workers and clients.

And yet, the questions persisted: "How can I serve more? How can I help more people?" I stopped focusing on the questions and just moved through my life experiences. Then, during a spiritual retreat in Tybee Island, Georgia, I threw the question out to the Atlantic Ocean. The answer was clear: "Write and teach about your spiritual experiences, faith and oncology massage. Write in Brazil." The warm feeling flooded all the cells in my body. I knew I would be moving to Brazil.

I wish I could tell you my faith was immediate, that I had no more questions. But I had doubts and questions. Why was I being moved away from a life filled with wonderful family and friends? Was I deserting my aging parents with their uncertain health conditions, as well as my oncology-massage clients? Couldn't I at least move to a country whose language I spoke?

But my spirit knew the answer was right. I opened myself up more to divine understanding and the all-knowing presence in my life. I let go.

It took two years of practical activities, such as clearing my finances, selling and giving away my possessions, emptying my beautiful house, preparing my family and friends, and learning a new language before I moved to Ilhabela, Brazil.

Some of my old friendships faltered as we all struggled with this gigantic change. Other relationships flourished, took wings and soared to new heights. There were doubts and fears hidden behind the most unsuspecting doors. I moved on in faith.

It was worth it. Ilhabela is the home of my heart. A beautiful island off the northern coast of Sao, Paulo, Ilhabela has wonderful beaches, a perfect climate, serenity, colorful wildlife, natural trails and abundant waterfalls.

Here, my words flow like the Amazon River, fluidly, freely. I am awakened by the neighborhood rooster and throw my bedroom window open to be greeted by beautiful, lush tropics. My eyes are nourished by a feast of colors: deep green fronds of coconut palms, vibrant reds and yellows of hibiscus trees. Here, my writing about my experiences with the oncology-massage clients I touched lovingly synergizes and flows from my fingers.

I write about the spiritual law of attraction that is ever-present in my life, about my experiences here in Brazil offering free massages to older adults underneath the 100-year- old mango tree, about free massages for oncology patients and about teaching oncology massage (in Portuguese, with help from friends) to any therapist whose heart spirit is led to learn.

One day my ever-evolving dream will manifest and oncology patients and their loved ones will come from all round the world to experience massage, yoga, healthy whole foods and the abundance of natural beauty Ilhabela has to offer.

My thoughts over the years of abundance, serenity, love, compassion and Joy attracted to me this wonderful experience of living, working and writing in Brazil. I am surrounded by warm, loving, gracious and generous friends here in Brazil, the home of my heart.

Is your heart calling out for more? Does your spirit want to move? Deep inside yourself is your answer. Quiet yourself. Activate your faith. Tap into your spiritual self. Live your Now. Come on, find your Brazil and help change the world!

Reprint from: Massage Magazine. Issue 150. November 2008. Pages 106-107.

Affirmations

Even the most tenacious leaf has to yield to the strong wind of change!
Change comes to move you *to* and *through* the next set of higher experiences in your life.

All of my steps are ordered by God!
I know that God orders my steps each day.

Jump in with both feet!
I embrace my spiritual good with a sense of vibrancy, Joy, and anticipation! I am eager for my Spiritual Good!

I surround myself with bright and beautiful things!
The things that surround me enliven and enrich my inner world.

I am Regenerated and Rejuvenated!
As my body heals, every cell in my body is regenerated
and rejuvenated in the most positive and healthy way.

I think my body well.
My thoughts are now
tuned into perfect
health and perfect healing.

Vase of Flowers

Healing Is a Journey

We all live in a human body. This miraculous creation of complicated systems enfolds our spirits. It is a blessing to have a body that is set for instant repair, instant compensation and instant self-correction. The things that our bodies can do are amazing.

We, as human beings, are surprised when our bodies go into self-healing. Our physical selves begin the healing process the instant our minds register the signal that something traumatic has happened. If you break a bone and fail to have a physician set and brace the bone properly, it will still begin its healing process. The results may not be as aesthetically pleasing or the bone may not function as well as before the injury, but the body heals.

Healing is inevitable. Healing is a journey. The healing path is as unique as there are unique personalities. Each one of us has our own special healing journey. Some of us will experience very few incidences of illness or injury, while others will seem to be in a constant state of poor health.

There are choices that we can make along our personal healing journey. We can choose to first treat our bodies well so that they are healthy and strong. We can exercise and strengthen our bones and muscles, eat nutritious foods, breathe deeply, rest, engage our minds in healthy, life-inspiring activities, and radiate love out to all we meet.

When our bodies need extra care, we can choose the medical or health professional that best resonates with our spirit. Talk to your friends and family members to find that physician who takes the time to connect with you.

Explore complementary and alternative therapies as healthy additions to your personal healing journey. And remember to surround yourself with people full of loving energy. Love activates and supports the healing journey in the best possible way.

It is also important to know and accept that within each of us is a deep well of healing energy. In fact, we are that well of perfect health. Give yourself permission to move through life as whole and healthy as you desire. We can create perfect health and wholeness for ourselves whenever we want. It is just a thought away. You truly deserve to experience the very best in your spirit, mind, emotions and body.

Healing with Colors

Color has been used for thousands of years to uplift emotions, cleanse and purify, renew and heal. Colors have a special spiritual healing message. Use the following pages to create your personal healing sessions.

Practicing these affirmations is very simple. Begin with Day 1. Find a quiet space. Allow your mind to open to these healing words. Choose a color that attracts you. Breathe deeply and read the affirmation. Exhale. Take another deep breath and imagine that the color is flowing through your body. Sit with your eyes closed for a few minutes in your color breathing in and out deeply.

You may focus on the beautiful artistic symbol on the page that expresses your color if you choose. Or you may close your eyes and imagine your color in your mind flowing and healing the different parts of the body. Each day focuses on a special part of your body. Day 7 brings your self-healing to the cellular level.

These affirmations may be used as often as you like. They are simple, powerful and effective. Allow yourself to feel and be well. Remember, we can tap into that unlimited supply of perfect health and well-being whenever we choose.

Affirmations
Healing Colors—7-Days

BLUE

Day 1 My healing color is **Blue** Today! I breathe in the color blue. Blue is peaceful and spiritual unfolding.

Day 2 I breathe the color blue into my heart and chest.

Day 3 I breathe the color blue into my solar plexus.

Day 4 I breathe the color blue into my arms and hands.

Day 5 I breathe the color blue into my legs and feet.

Day 6 I breathe the color blue into my head and hair.

Day 7 I breathe the color blue into my eyes.

I feel its healing presence now. Every cell in my body is healed with the color blue.

Healing Tree

YELLOW

Day 1 My healing color is **Yellow** today! I breathe in the color yellow. As I look at the color yellow, I know that my spirit is illuminating and expanding. I feel happy.

Day 2 I breathe the color yellow into my heart and chest.

Day 3 I breathe the color yellow into my solar plexus.

Day 4 I breathe the color yellow into my arms and hands.

Day 5 I breathe color yellow into my legs and feet.

Day 6 I breathe the color yellow into my head and hair.

Day 7 I breathe the color yellow into my eyes.

I absorb yellow's healing powers now. Every cell in my body is healed with the color yellow.

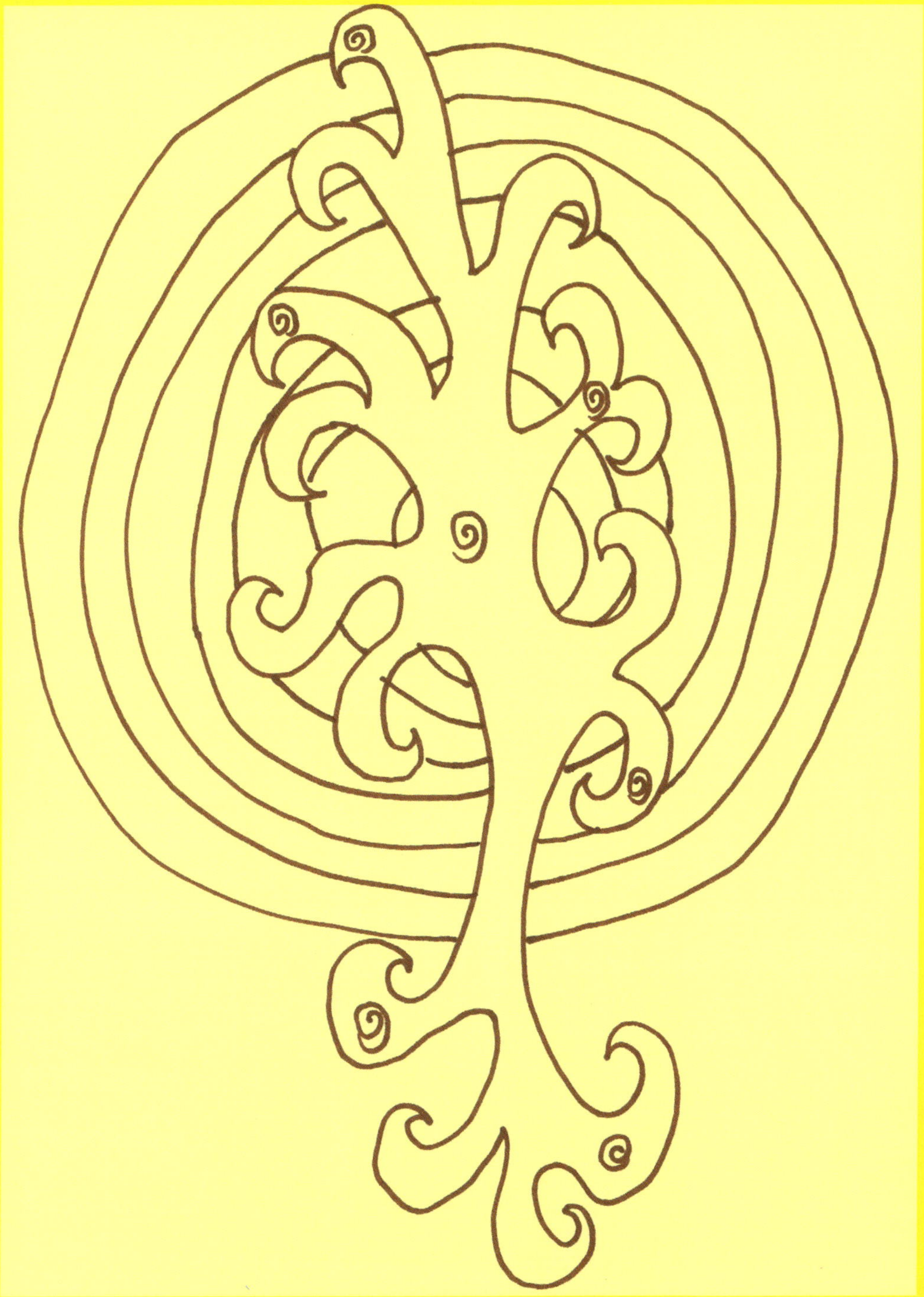

PINK

Day 1 My healing color is **Pink** today! Pink surrounds me with its power of love and protection.

Day 2 I breathe the color pink into my heart and chest.

Day 3 I breathe the color pink into my solar plexus.

Day 4 I breathe the color pink into my arms and hands.

Day 5 I breathe the color pink into my legs and feet.

Day 6 I breathe the color pink into my head and hair.

Day 7 I breathe the color pink into my eyes.

I absorb the healing color of pink into my body now. Every cell in my body is healed with the color pink.

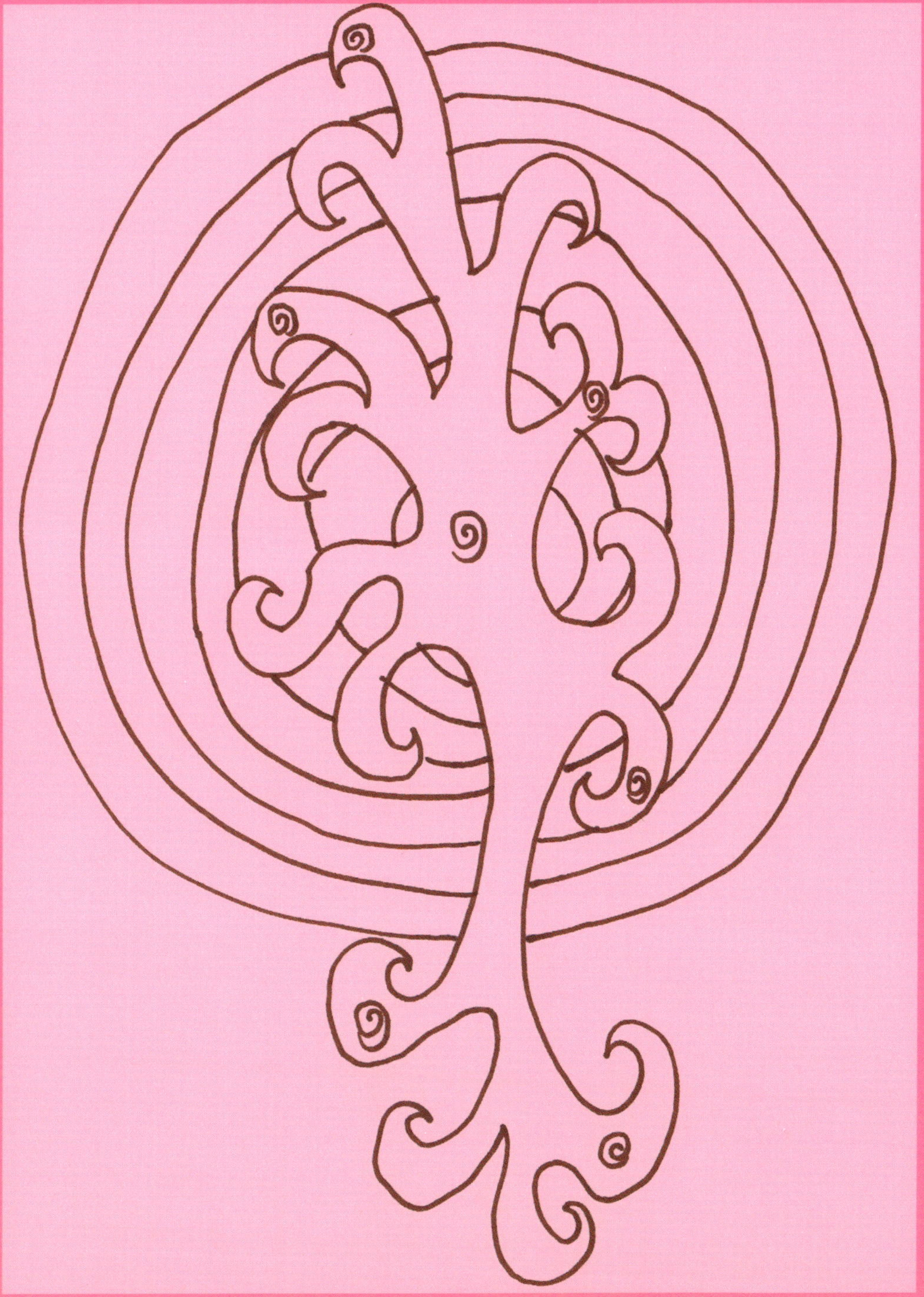

ORANGE

Day 1 My healing color is **Orange** today! When I see the color orange my soul feels happy. The color orange stimulates positive energy in my life.

Day 2 I breathe the color orange into my heart and chest.

Day 3 I breathe the color orange into my solar plexus.

Day 4 I breathe the color orange into my arms and hands.

Day 5 I breathe the color orange into my legs and feet.

Day 6 I breathe the color orange into my head and hair.

Day 7 I breathe the color orange into my eyes.

I absorb the color orange into my body and activate perfect healing now. Every cell in my body is healed with the color orange.

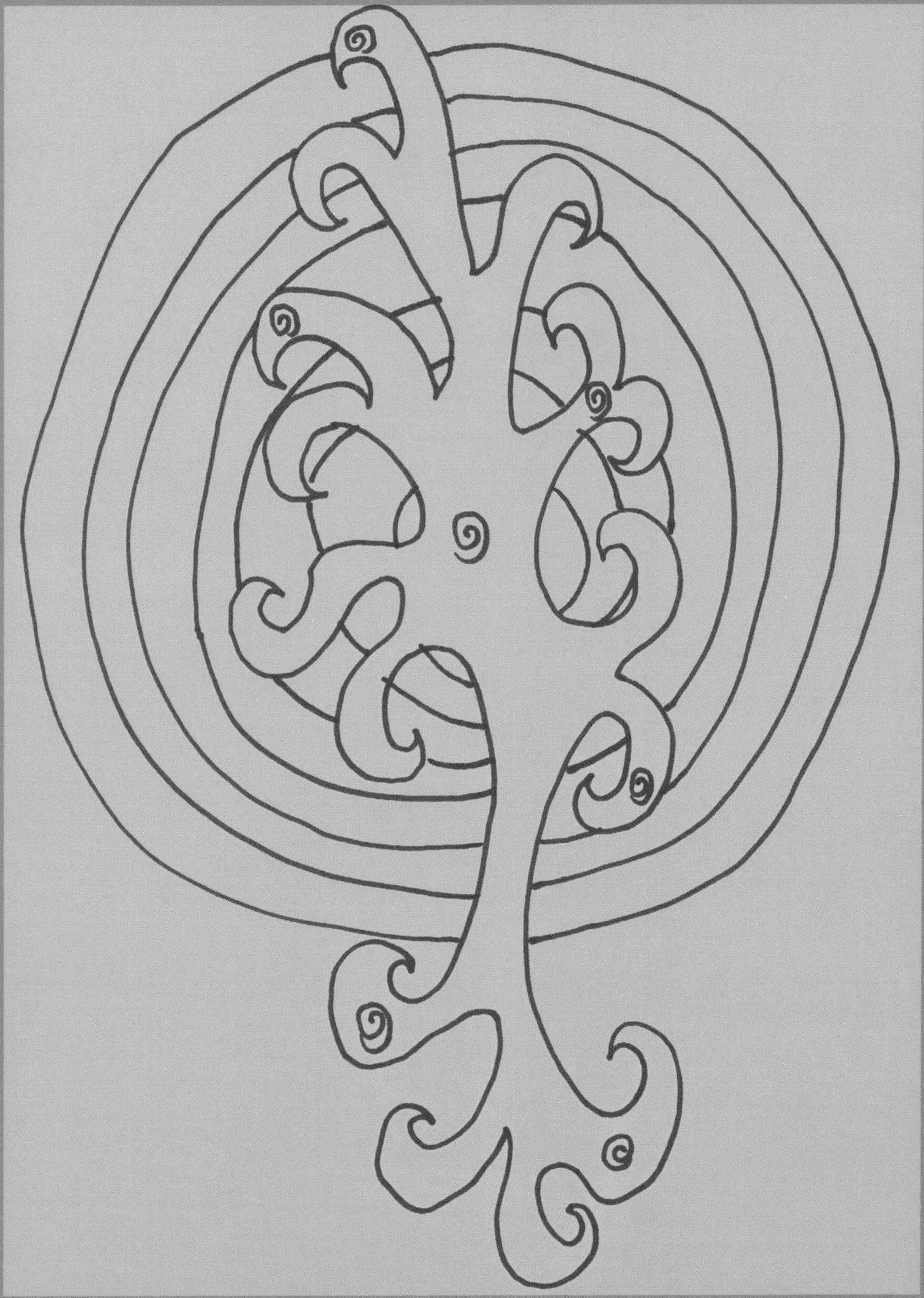

RED

Day 1 My healing color is **Red** today! Red represents my passion for life! The color red stimulates prosperity in my life today.

Day 2 I breathe the color red into my heart and chest.

Day 3 I breathe the color red into my solar plexus.

Day 4 I breathe the color red into my arms and hands.

Day 5 I breathe the color red into my legs and feet.

Day 6 I breathe the color red into my head and hair.

Day 7 I breathe the color red into my eyes.

My cells are revitalized by the color red. Every cell in my body is healed with the color red.

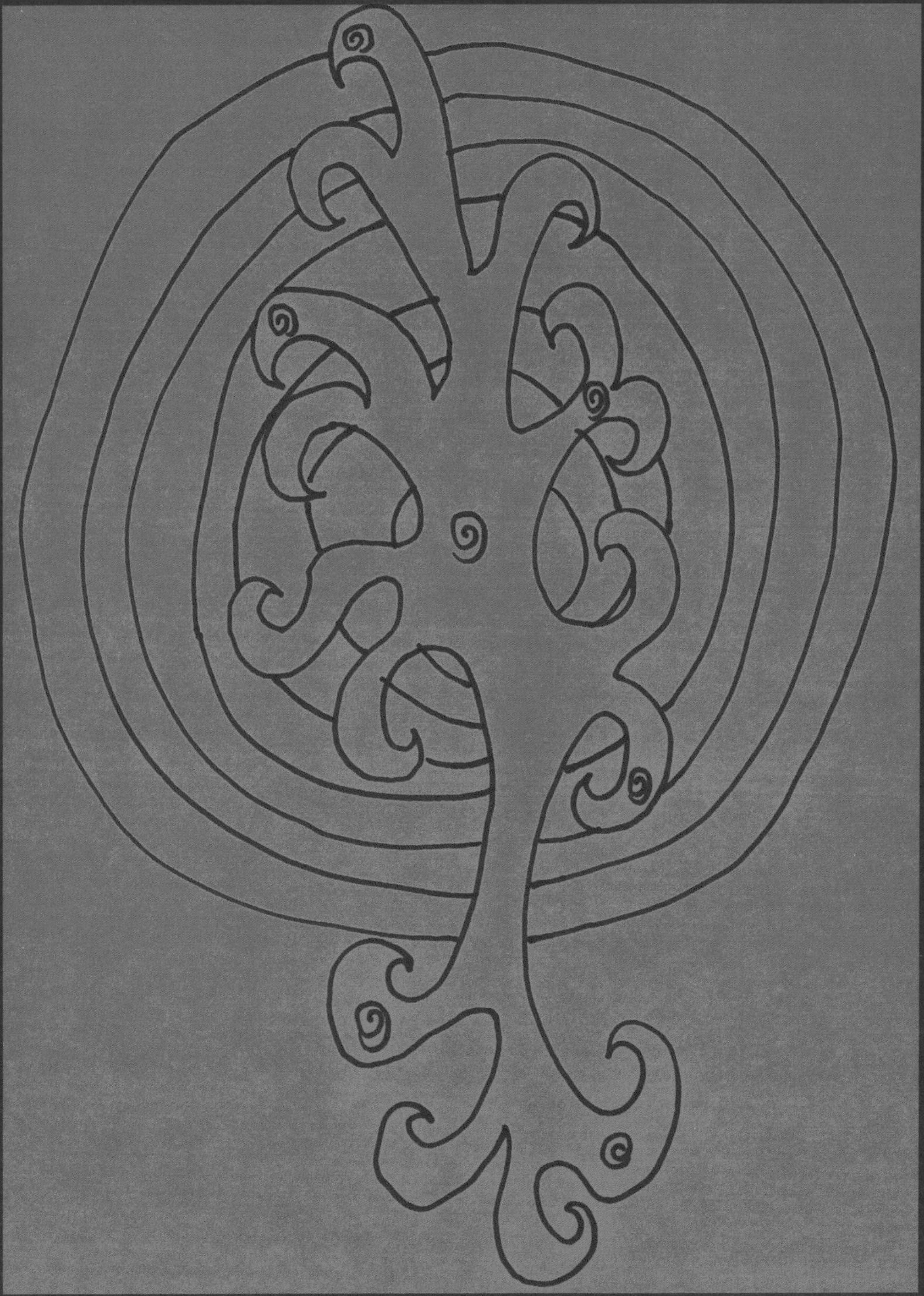

GREEN

Day 1 My healing color is **Green** today! The color green brings my body, mind, and spirit into perfect balance. The color green reminds me that I am one with nature.

Day 2 I breathe the color green into my heart and chest.

Day 3 I breathe the color green into my solar plexus.

Day 4 I breathe the color green into my arms and hands.

Day 5 I breathe the color green into my legs and feet.

Day 6 I breathe the color green into my head and hair.

Day 7 I breathe the color green into my eyes.

I absorb the color green into my body and activate perfect healing now. Every cell in my body is healed with the color green.

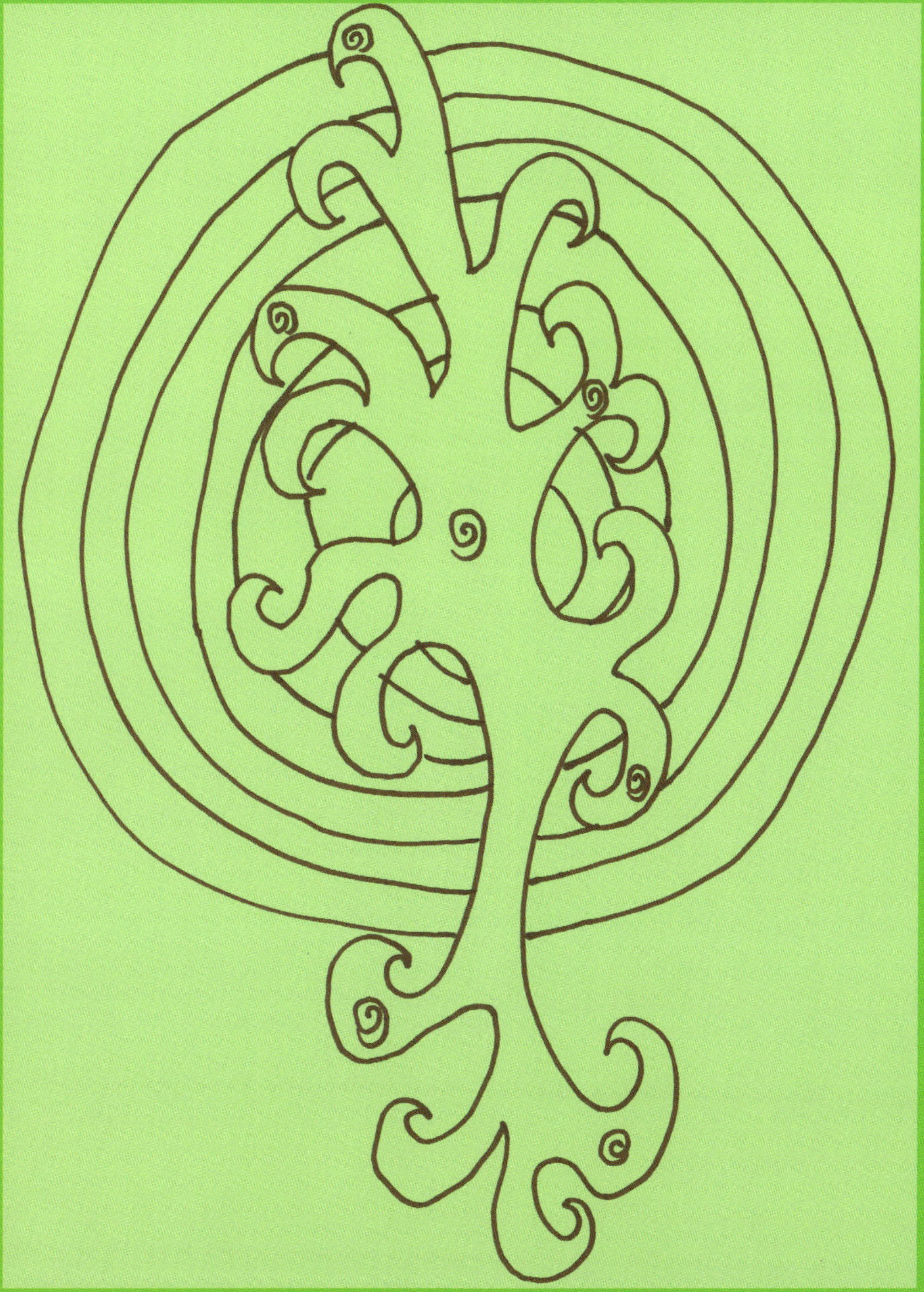

WHITE

Day 1 My healing color is **White** today! I use the healing powers of the color white today to cleanse, purify, and enlighten my mind, spirit, and body.

Day 2 I breathe the color white into my heart and chest.

Day 3 I breathe the color white into my solar plexus.

Day 4 I breathe the color white into my arms and hands.

Day 5 I breathe the color white into my legs and feet.

Day 6 I breathe the color white into my head and hair.

Day 7 I breathe the color white into my eyes.

The color white brings spiritual healing to my body. Every cell in my body is healed with the color white.

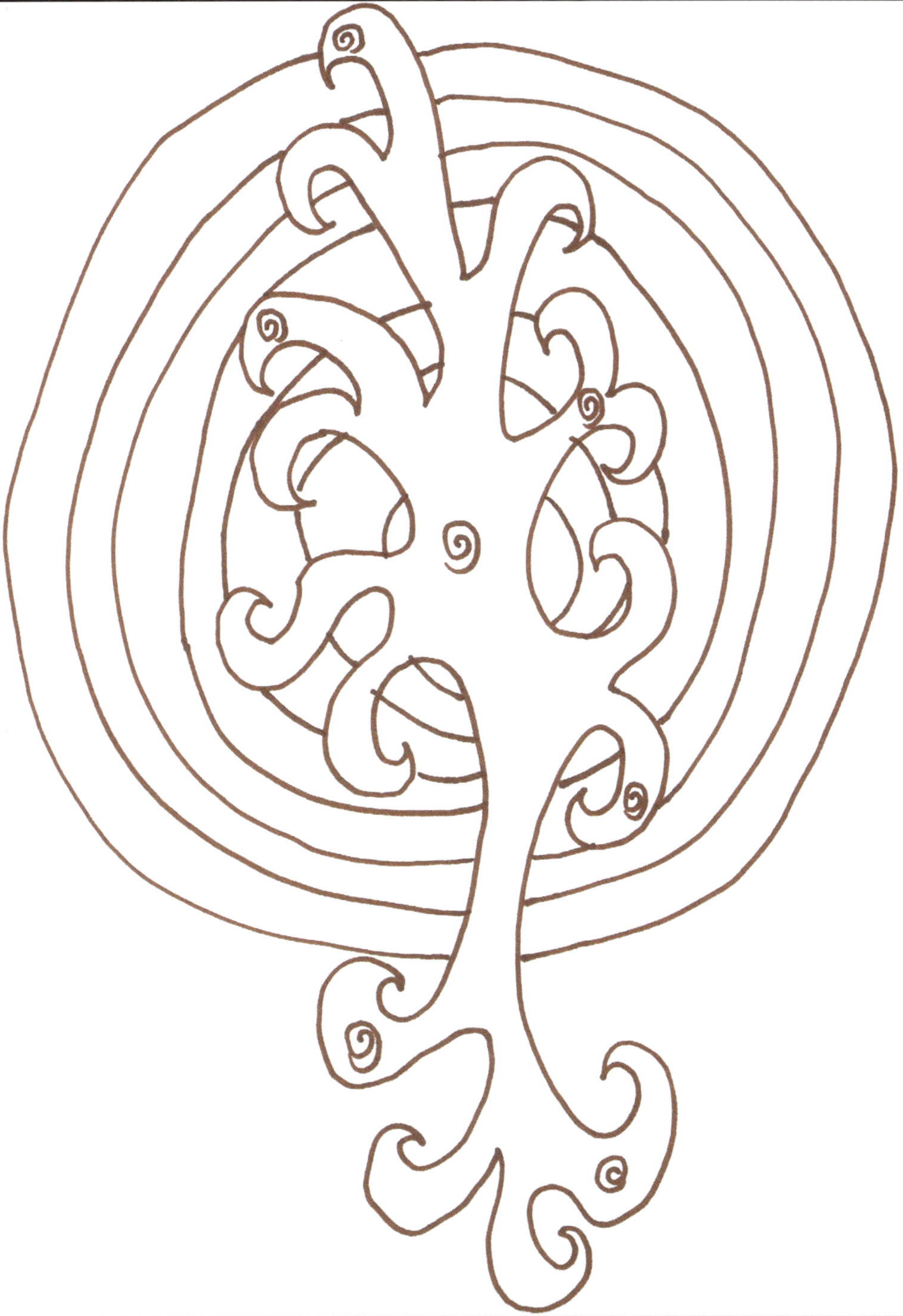

PURPLE

Day 1 My healing color is **Purple** today! Purple is intuitive and meditative. When I see the color purple my body intuitively knows exactly what is perfect for self-healing.

Day 2 I breathe the color purple into my heart and chest.

Day 3 I breathe the color purple into my solar plexus.

Day 4 I breathe the color purple into my arms and hands.

Day 5 I breathe the color purple into my legs and feet.

Day 6 I breathe the color purple into my head and hair.

Day 7 I breathe the color purple into my eyes.

I feel purple's healing presence in my body now. Every cell in my body is healed with the color purple.

Each and every part of me works together perfectly creating a healthier, happier, me!

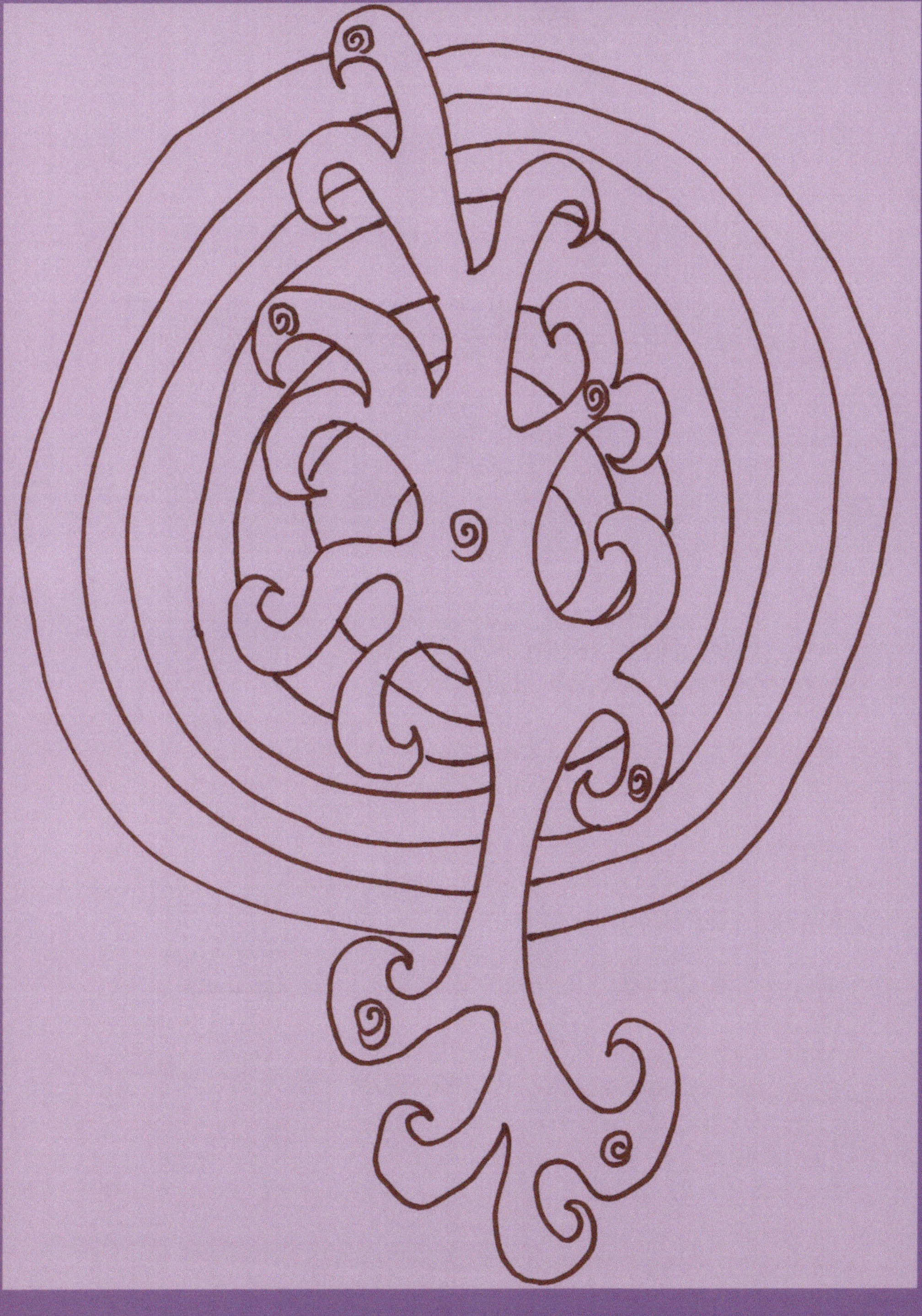

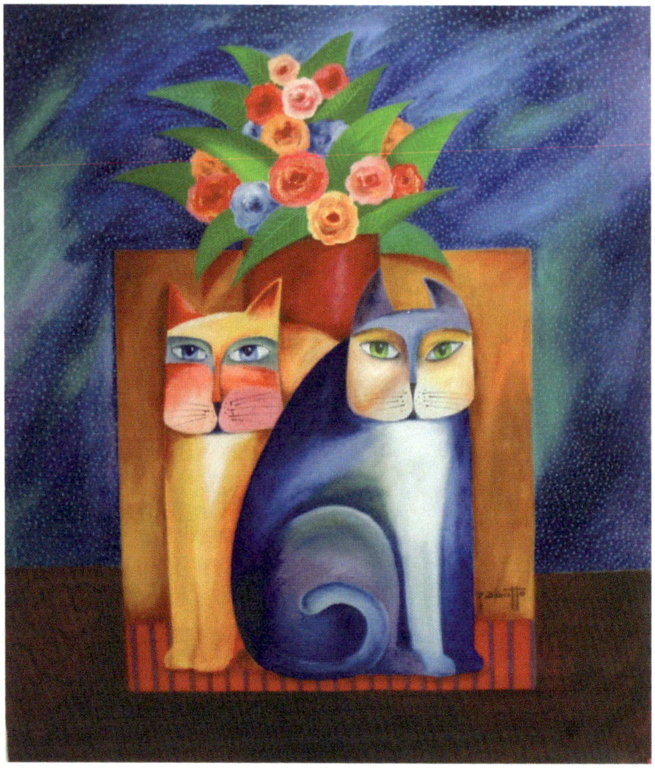

About the Author

Vickie D. Torrey is a counselor, licensed massage and bodywork therapist, writer, mystic traveler and teacher. Her passion for massage and holistic health led her to establish Lighten Up Holistic Health Service, an international health and training agency for both adults and children. She taught massage and movement at Omega Institute of Holistic Studies in Rhinebeck, New York. Vickie has also found great joy in working with people who have experienced domestic violence and abuse, teaching them the power of healing touch.

While working in a regional hospital system, Vickie compassionately touched the lives of persons experiencing HIV/AIDs, Parkinson's disease, Multiple Sclerosis, Polio, ALS and Cancer. That experience led her to specialize in oncology massage which she now teaches nationally and internationally. As an international teacher, Vickie is also a faculty member at Costa Rica School of Massage Therapy in Samara Beach, Costa Rica.

Vickie lives in Charlotte, N.C. and Ilhabela, São Paulo, Brazil the home of her heart where she writes, teaches and plays. She is the mother of two beautiful daughters, Diarra and Serena. She has written for *The Charlotte Post*, *Medicine & Science In Sport & Exercise*, and *Massage Magazine*.

Photograph by Noreda Hess

Contact Vickie at:
healing.spirits@yahoo.com
mystichandshealingspirits.blogspot.com
liveloveheal.org
Facebook

Meet the Artists

Flavio Zabotto

My friend Flavio Zabotto was born in an Italian family from the Veneto region of northern Italy that immigrated to Brazil because of the coffee plantation boom. The Zabotto family left the coffee plantation and moved to São Paulo in the early 1950's.

A self-taught artist who created his own personal style of artistic expression, Flavio's life path took him from living on a coffee plantation to working in a major textile factory in São Paulo. Flavio spent 25 years mastering the art of commercial textile art and design in this major city. Yet painting and full artistic expression continued to call his spirit, so in 1996 Flavio left his management job and moved to the island of Ilhabela, Brazil.

I met Flavio in Ilhabela. Curious about the new American neighbor but unable to speak sufficient English, Flavio persuaded friends to introduce us. Our friendship was instant. We are spiritual family. We did not allow language to become a barrier to developing our life-long friendship.

Flavio Zabotto's art and paintings are well-known and well-received by a growing number of galleries, collectors, decorators, and international tourists. Flavio's artistic expression is vibrant, passionate, soulful, enthusiastic, joyful and sometimes humorous. It truly pulls you in to experience it and to experience this amazing adventure called life to the fullest!

I encourage you to learn more about Flavio's life and art by visiting his web pages at:

www.flickr.com/photos/zabottogallery

www.picasaweb.com/google/zabottogallery

flaviozabotto.blogspot.com

f.zabotto@hotmail.com

Photo by Ronald Kraag

Cynthia J. Allison

Cynthia J. Allison is the artist who created the Healing Tree that beautifully illustrates the color healing meditations. She and I became family while working as team members of Carolinas Integrative Health in Charlotte, North Carolina. Inspired by our vision, Cynthia created an amazing artistic tree that symbolized all of the modalities and services we offered.

Cynthia has a wonderful spiritual connection to trees. She often sees life as a tree with roots symbolizing being grounded and branches expressing spiritual expansion. Her tree art ranges from quirky to deeply soulful. Cynthia's own soul expression is Joy.

Highly creative and open to being on her spiritual path, Cynthia sees each moment in life as an opportunity to learn and create. She has an extensive art and music background, a passion that began at an early age. She is an emerging artist who is currently expanding her freelance art business.

Cynthia J. Allison lives in Charlotte, North Carolina where she works, plays, paints and adores her beautiful new baby daughter, Arianna Giselle.

You may contact her at:

smilinghappyfrog@yahoo.com

Photo by Vickie Torrey

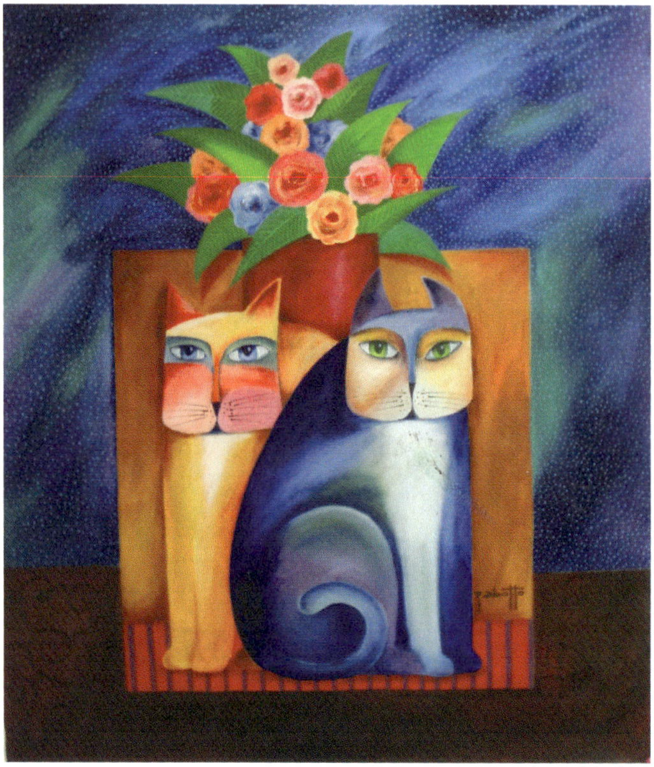

Bibliography

Chopra, Deepak. *Power Freedom and Grace: Living from the Source of Lasting Happiness.* San Rafeal, California: Amber-Allen Publishing, Inc., 2006.

Thurman, Robert. *The Jewel of Tibet.* New York: Simon and Schuster, Inc., 2005.

Williamson, Marianne. *A Return to Love.* (New York: HarperCollins Publishers, 1996), 65.

CPSIA information can be obtained
at www.ICGtesting.com
226556LV00001B